CHICKEN
DISHES

HAMLYN

COOK'S NOTES

OVEN TEMPERATURES

°C	°F	GAS MARK	
70 C	150 F	Low	–
80 C	175 F	Low	–
90 C	190 F	Low	–
100 C	200 F	¼	–
110 C	225 F	¼	Very slow
130 C	250 F	½	Very slow
150 C	275 F	1	Slow
160 C	300 F	2	Moderately slow
170 C	325 F	3	Moderately slow
180 C	350 F	4	Moderate
190 C	375 F	5	Moderately hot
200 C	400 F	6	Hot
220 C	425 F	7	Hot
230 C	450 F	8	Very hot
240 C	475 F	9	Very hot

MICROWAVE POWER SETTINGS

Power Level	Percentage	Numerical Setting
HIGH	100%	9
MEDIUM HIGH	75%	7
MEDIUM	50%	5
DEFROST	30%	3
LOW	10%	1

SOLID WEIGHT CONVERSIONS

METRIC	IMPERIAL
15 g	½ oz
25 g	1 oz
50 g	2 oz
100 g	4 oz/¼ lb
175 g	6 oz
225 g	8 oz/½ lb
350 g	12 oz
450 g	1 lb
575 g	1¼ lb
700 g	1½ lb
800 g	1¾ lb
900 g	2 lb

MICROWAVE

Microwave tips have been tested using a 650 watt microwave oven. Add 15 seconds per minute for 600 watt ovens and reduce the timings by 5-10 seconds per minute for 700 watt ovens.

LIQUID VOLUME CONVERSIONS

METRIC	IMPERIAL
25 ml	1 fl oz
50 ml	2 fl oz
125 ml	4 fl oz
150 ml	5 fl oz/¼ pt
175 ml	6 fl oz
225 ml	8 fl oz
300 ml	10 fl oz/½ pt
450 ml	15 fl oz/¾ pt
600 ml	20 fl oz/1pt
900 ml	1½ pt
1.2 l	2 pt
1.7 l	3 pt

AUSTRALIAN CUP CONVERSIONS

	METRIC	IMP
1 cup flour	150 g	5 oz
1 cup sugar, granulated	225 g	8 oz
1 cup sugar, caster	225 g	8 oz
1 cup sugar, icing	175 g	6 oz
1 cup sugar, soft brown	175 g	6 oz
1 cup butter	225 g	8 oz
1 cup honey, treacle	350 g	12 oz
1 cup fresh breadcrumbs	50 g	2 oz
1 cup uncooked rice	200 g	7 oz
1 cup dried fruit	175 g	6 oz
1 cup chopped nuts	100 g	4 oz
1 cup desiccated coconut	75 g	3 oz
1 cup liquid	250 ml	9 fl oz

WEIGHTS AND MEASURES

Metric and Imperial weights and measures are given throughout. Don't switch from one to the other within a recipe as they are not interchangeable. 1 tsp is the equivalent of a 5 ml spoon and 1 tbls equals a 15 ml spoon.

All spoon measurements are level, all flour plain, all sugar granulated and all eggs medium unless otherwise stated.

SYMBOLS

 FREEZER TIP

 SERVING SUGGESTION

 MICRO-WAVE TIP

 WINE & DRINK NOTE

CONTENTS

First published in Great Britain in 1993 by Hamlyn
an imprint of Reed Consumer Books Limited
Michelin House, 81 Fulham Road, London SW3 6RB
and Auckland, Melbourne, Singapore and Toronto

Reprinted 1993, 1994 (twice)

ISBN 0 600 57776 7

A CIP catalogue record for this book is available from the British Library

Produced by Mandarin Offset
Printed and bound in Singapore

CHICKEN SATAY WITH PEANUT SAUCE

James Duncan

Indonesian and Thai restaurants are popping
up all over the country and this is one
of their most popular dishes. The crunchy,
spicy peanut sauce can also be served as a dip.

PREPARATION TIME: 15 MINS
+ MARINATING
COOKING TIME: 25 MINS
SERVES 4-6

INGREDIENTS

700 G/1 LB 8 OZ CHICKEN BREASTS,
CUT INTO 2 CM/³⁄₄ IN CUBES

FOR THE MARINADE

1 SMALL ONION, SLICED

50 ML/2 FL OZ PEANUT OIL

1 TSP CORIANDER SEEDS, CRUSHED

½ TSP FENNEL SEEDS, CRUSHED

2 CARDAMOM PODS, CRUSHED

2 ALLSPICE, CRUSHED

½ TSP GARAM MASALA

PINCH OF SALT

1 LEMON

CURLY ENDIVE, TO GARNISH

FOR THE PEANUT SAUCE

1 TBLS GROUNDNUT OIL

1 SMALL ONION, FINELY DICED

1 CLOVE OF GARLIC, CRUSHED

25 G/1 OZ FRESH GINGER, PEELED
AND GRATED

100 G/4 OZ CRUNCHY PEANUT
BUTTER

150 ML/¼ PT CHICKEN STOCK

50 G/2 OZ COCONUT CREAM

JUICE OF ½ LIME

SALT AND GROUND BLACK PEPPER

CARROT SLIVERS, TO GARNISH

2 Drain the cubes of chicken reserving the marinated onion. Thread onto satay sticks.

3 Make the peanut sauce: heat the oil in a heavy saucepan. Add the onion, garlic and ginger and fry for 5 minutes over a low heat until soft. Add the peanut butter, chicken stock and coconut cream and cook, stirring constantly, until blended. Liquidise the sauce, add the lime juice and season with salt and black pepper. Garnish the sauce with slivers of carrot.

4 Heat the barbecue or grill to high. Grill the kebabs for 12 minutes. Turn halfway through and baste with the marinade.

1 Make the marinade: mix the onion, peanut oil, coriander, fennel, cardamom pods, allspice, garam masala and salt together. Pare the lemon skin and finely slice. Squeeze the juice and add both to the marinade. Put the chicken into a mixing bowl and pour the marinade over the top. Cover this with cling film and marinate in the fridge overnight.

5 To serve, transfer the kebabs to a heated serving platter, scatter the marinated onion over the top and garnish with curly endive. Serve immediately with the warm peanut sauce.

TIP

ADD 1 TSP CHOPPED LEMON GRASS TO THE
MARINADE FOR EXTRA FLAVOUR.

CHICKEN & PEPPER BAKE

Clint Brown

Homely chicken bake is given a continental feel, thanks to the colourful layer of sliced green peppers. Serve with a mixed salad.

PREPARATION TIME: 15 MINS
COOKING TIME: 55 MINS
SERVES 4-6

INGREDIENTS

3 GREEN PEPPERS, CORED AND
SEEDED

1 LARGE ONION

4 TBLS OIL

1 CLOVE OF GARLIC, PEELED AND
CRUSHED

4 CHICKEN BREASTS, BONED AND
SKINNED

1 TBLS FLOUR

1 TBLS CHOPPED FRESH PARSLEY

1 TBLS CHOPPED FRESH OREGANO

150 ML/¼ PT STRONG CHICKEN
STOCK

300 ML/½ PT DOUBLE CREAM

GRATED ZEST OF HALF A LEMON

2 EGG YOLKS, BEATEN

SALT AND GROUND BLACK PEPPER

¼ TSP GROUND NUTMEG

75 G/3 OZ PARMESAN CHEESE,
GRATED

2 Add remaining oil to the pan and heat. Cut chicken into 2.5 cm/1 in pieces and add to pan. Cook for 5 minutes, until browned. Gradually stir in the flour and cook for 2 minutes. Add the herbs and stock. Bring to the boil. Remove from heat.

3 Arrange a layer of peppers and onions in the bottom of a large ovenproof dish. Top with the chicken and peppers.

1 Preheat the oven to 160 C/300 F/ Gas 2. Thinly slice peppers and onion. Heat 2 tbls of the oil in a frying-pan and cook the peppers for 10 minutes, until softened.Remove from the pan with a slotted spoon. Add the onion and garlic and cook for 5 minutes to soften. Remove from pan.

4 Stir the cream, lemon zest, egg yolks, salt, pepper and nutmeg together in a bowl and pour over the meat. Sprinkle with the cheese. Bake in the oven for 35 minutes. Remove from the heat and serve.

CHICKEN KORMA

Diana Miller

Chicken Korma is a favourite at Indian restaurants, but next time you fancy an Indian meal don't go out – stay in and try this easy-to- follow recipe instead.

PREPARATION TIME: 20 MINS
COOKING TIME: 45 MINS
SERVES 4-6

I N G R E D I E N T S

700 G/1 ½ LB CHICKEN BREASTS	
100 G/4 OZ GROUND ALMONDS	
4 CM/1 ½ IN PIECE OF FRESH GINGER, PEELED AND ROUGHLY SLICED	
1 LARGE CLOVE OF GARLIC, PEELED	
2 FRESH GREEN CHILLIES, SEEDED	
2 TBLS GHEE OR VEGETABLE OIL	
1 ONION, CHOPPED	
½ TSP TURMERIC POWDER	
4 GREEN CARDAMOM PODS	
4 CLOVES	
2.5 CM/1 IN PIECE OF CINNAMON STICK	
1 TSP CORIANDER SEEDS	
1 TSP CUMIN SEEDS	
1 TSP CORNFLOUR	
225 G/8 OZ GREEK STRAINED YOGHURT	
JUICE OF ½ LEMON	
2 TBLS CORIANDER, CHOPPED	
25 G/1 OZ CREAMED COCONUT	
SALT	

2 Heat the ghee or vegetable oil in a large frying-pan and fry the onion over a moderate heat until lightly coloured. Add the turmeric, cardamom, cloves, cinnamon, coriander and cumin seeds. Fry for 1 minute.

3 Mix the cornflour with the yoghurt. Return the frying-pan to the heat and gradually add the yoghurt mixture, mixing well.

4 Add the nut paste, 50 ml/2 fl oz water and the chicken and bring to simmering point. Simmer for 30 minutes or until the chicken is cooked through.

5 Add the lemon juice, chopped coriander, creamed coconut and salt to taste. Heat for 1 minute to dissolve the coconut, then serve.

TIP

GHEE IS A KIND OF CLARIFIED BUTTER USED IN INDIAN COOKING. IF YOU DON'T HAVE ANY USE VEGETABLE OIL INSTEAD.

SERVE CHICKEN KORMA WITH SOME FRESH-COOKED RICE FLECKED WITH RED CHILLI AND A BOWL OF MANGO CHUT-NEY. GARNISH WITH EXTRA CHOPPED CORIANDER.

1 Skin the chicken and cut into 2.5 cm/1 in cubes. Put the almonds, ginger, garlic and chillies in a blender with 150 ml/¼ pt cold water and blend to a paste.

CHICKEN BIRYANI

Clint Brown

Many cooks think Indian food is too complicated to try. This recipe – all cooked in one pan – will show you just how wrong that theory is.

PREPARATION TIME: 10 MINS
COOKING TIME: 30-35 MINS
SERVES 4

I N G R E D I E N T S

50 G/2 OZ BUTTER
2½ CM/1 IN PIECE OF FRESH GINGER, GRATED
2 CLOVES OF GARLIC, CRUSHED
5 CM/2 IN CINNAMON STICK
1 TBLS CORIANDER SEEDS, CRUSHED
2 CARDAMOM PODS, CRUSHED
3 CLOVES
2 TSP GROUND CUMIN
4 CHICKEN BREASTS, SLICED
1 LARGE ONION, SLICED
350-400 G/12-14 OZ BASMATI RICE
1.2 L/2 PT CHICKEN STOCK
PINCH OF SAFFRON
1 BAY LEAF
½ TSP GRATED NUTMEG
50 G/2 OZ PISTACHIO NUTS
50 G/2 OZ RAISINS
TO SERVE
1 LARGE ONION, SLICED INTO RINGS
OIL, FOR FRYING
FRESH CORIANDER SPRIGS

from the pan when lightly browned. Add the onion and sauté for 2 minutes. Stir in the rice and coat with the spices. Cover with chicken stock, add the saffron strands and bay leaf and bring to the boil, stirring occasionally.

2 Lay the chicken strips on top of the rice mixture, cover and simmer for 15 minutes. Stir in the nutmeg, pistachio nuts and raisins, and cook for a further 10-15 minutes until the rice is tender.

3 Fry the onion rings in the oil until well-browned and crisp. Garnish the biryani with the onion rings. and fresh coriander sprigs.

SERVE THIS BIRYANI WITH SIDE DISHES OF CHUTNEY AND NAAN BREAD.

1 Melt the butter and stir in the ginger, garlic and spices. Quickly fry the chicken strips and remove

NUNG PAO CHICKEN

Hilary Moore

Tender chicken chunks combine with crunchy
nuts to create this tasty Szechwan dish.

PREPARATION TIME: 40 MINS
+ MARINATING
COOKING TIME: 10 MINS
SERVES 4

INGREDIENTS

450 G/1 LB CHICKEN BREAST, BONED

FOR THE MARINADE

½ TSP SALT

GROUND BLACK PEPPER

1 TBLS SHAO HSING WINE OR SHERRY

1 TBLS LIGHT SOY SAUCE

1 TBLS LIGHTLY BEATEN EGG WHITE

FOR THE SAUCE

1 TBLS DARK SOY SAUCE

1 TBLS WHITE WINE VINEGAR

2 TBLS CHILLI SAUCE

2 TSP SUGAR

2 TSP CORNFLOUR

6 TBLS CHICKEN STOCK

4 TBLS GROUNDNUT OIL

1 LONG RED CHILLI SEEDED AND CUT INTO SMALL PIECES

2.5 CM/1 IN ROOT GINGER, PEELED AND SLICED

2 CLOVES OF GARLIC, PEELED AND SLICED

1 TBLS SHAO HSING WINE OR SHERRY

6 SPRING ONIONS, SLICED THINLY

50 G/2 OZ ROASTED PEANUTS OR CASHEW NUTS

3 Heat the oil in a wok until hot, add the chilli, ginger and garlic and fry for 2 minutes stirring constantly to cook evenly and prevent burning.

4 Add the chicken and cook over a high heat for 5 minutes, stir in the Shao hsing wine or sherry and spring onions, cook for a further minute.

1 Cut the chicken into 2.5 cm/1 in cubes and place in a bowl. Add the seasoning, Shao hsing wine or sherry, soy sauce and egg white. Stir well until thoroughly mixed, cover and leave to marinate for 30 minutes.

2 Mix the dark soy sauce, white wine vinegar, chilli sauce, sugar, cornflour and stock in a jug. Set aside to use later.

5 Pour in the mixed sauce and stir until thickened, just before serving stir in the roasted peanuts or cashew nuts and serve.

PASTA RING WITH PESTO CHICKEN

Alan Newnham

This is a delightful dish for an *al fresco* lunch,
using two favourites – chicken and pasta – to
make an unusual centre-piece.

14

PREPARATION TIME: 30 MINS +
CHILLING
COOKING TIME: 8-12 MINS
SERVES 6

I N G R E D I E N T S

450 G/1 LB THIN RIBBON PASTA

1 PIECE OF TINNED RED PIMIENTO,
FINELY SLICED

3 TBLS VINAIGRETTE DRESSING

1.4–1.6 KG/3-3 LB 8 OZ CHICKEN,
POACHED AND CUT INTO SMALL
PIECES

FLAT-LEAVED PARSLEY, TO GARNISH

FOR THE PESTO SAUCE

i OO G/4 OZ PINE KERNELS

LARGE HANDFUL OF BASIL OR
PARSLEY

2 LARGE CLOVES OF GARLIC

75 ML/3 FL OZ OLIVE OIL

SALT AND GROUND BLACK PEPPER

2 Bring a large pan of well-salted water to the boil. Cook the pasta until *al dente* – soft but still firm, approximately 8-12 minutes. Drain in a colander then pour a pan or kettle of boiling water over to rinse.

3 In a large bowl, mix together the pasta, sliced pimiento and vinaigrette dressing. Taste and season. Press the pasta into a large ring mould and chill for at least 1 hour.

1 First make the pesto sauce: place the pine kernels, herbs and garlic in a food processor and grind to a fine paste. Add the oil and seasoning and blend. Alternatively, finely chop the nuts and herbs, place in a mortar with the garlic and work to a paste with a pestle. Work in the oil and seasoning.

4 Mix the pesto sauce with the pieces of chicken. Carefully turn the pasta ring out onto a serving platter and fill the centre with the chicken. Garnish with flat-leaved parsley and serve.

SERVE PASTA RING WITH
PESTO CHICKEN ON A BED OF
LETTUCE WITH A TOMATO AND
BASIL SALAD.

TIP

USE A COMBINATION OF YELLOW, GREEN, RED OR WHOLEMEAL PASTA. CHECK THEY HAVE TO BE COOKED FOR THE SAME TIME: IF NOT, PUT THE ONES THAT TAKE LONGEST IN FIRST THEN ADD THE OTHERS AS NECESSARY. RINSE WITH BOILING WATER TO REMOVE STICKY STARCH.

TROPICAL CHICKEN

Michael Michaels

Here's an unusual way to serve chicken that not
only tastes tropical - it looks that way too.

PREPARATION TIME: 1 HOUR
COOKING TIME: 1 HOUR
SERVES 4

INGREDIENTS

| 4 COCONUTS |
| 3 BONED CHICKEN BREASTS, SKINNED |
| 3 RASHERS SMOKED BACK BACON |
| 2 TBLS SUNFLOWER OIL |
| 1 CLOVE OF GARLIC, CRUSHED |
| 2 ONIONS, CHOPPED |
| 2 GREEN PEPPERS, DICED |
| 225 G/8 OZ FROZEN SWEETCORN KERNELS |
| 6 TOMATOES, SKINNED |
| SALT AND GROUND BLACK PEPPER |

garlic, onions, green peppers and sweetcorn to the pan. Fry gently until onions and the other vegetables are softened but not browned.

3 Preheat the oven to 190 C/375 F/ Gas 5. Cut up the tomatoes and add to the vegetables. Return the meat to the pan with the chopped coconut. Season and bring to a boil, then divide among the coconuts. Cover with lids.

1 Strip away as many of the coconut fibres as possible. Using a thick nail or skewer, make three holes in top of each coconut and drain away the milk. Then saw off about 5 cm/2 in from the same end in which the holes have been made to make a lid. Using a sharp knife, remove some of the coconut flesh from the neck of each coconut, chop this flesh finely and set aside.

4 Loosely wrap each coconut in a piece of foil and stand each in a metal pastry cutter in a roasting tin so that the coconuts are upright. Pour in 2.5 cm/1 in hot water, bake for 1 hour. Remove the foil and serve in the shells, eating the coconut flesh if wished.

2 Cut the chicken into strips. Remove the bacon rind and cut the bacon into pieces. Heat the oil in a frying-pan and gently fry the chicken and bacon for 5-6 minutes until cooked. Remove the meat with a slotted spoon and then add the

TIP

SAWING OFF COCONUT TOPS IS QUITE HARD WORK. ALTERNATIVELY, YOU CAN USE THE FLESH OF HALF A COCONUT, AND SERVE THE CHICKEN IN BOWLS.

CHICKEN GUMBO WITH OKRA

Peter Reilly

For a hot and hearty family meal, serve this chicken gumbo with Arcadian potato salad.

PREPARATION TIME: 20 MINS
COOKING TIME: 1 HOUR 10 MINS
SERVES 6

I N G R E D I E N T S

2 TBLS OIL	
50 G/2 OZ BUTTER	
1.5 KG/3 LB CHICKEN, SKINNED AND QUARTERED	
175 G/6 OZ GAMMON, CUBED	
450 G/1 LB OKRA, TRIMMED	
450 G/1 LB TOMATOES, SKINNED AND CHOPPED	
2 LARGE ONIONS, CHOPPED	
1 GREEN PEPPER, SEEDED AND CUBED	
4 CELERY STALKS, TRIMMED AND CHOPPED	
2 TBLS CHOPPED FRESH CORIANDER	
2 TBLS CHOPPED FRESH PARSLEY	
3 BAY LEAVES	
1 TSP TURMERIC	
1 TBLS TOMATO PUREE	
SALT AND GROUND BLACK PEPPER	

1 Heat the oil and butter in a flameproof casserole, fry the chicken for 10 minutes until golden.

2 Add the gammon. Cook for 5 minutes. Add the vegetables, herbs and seasonings. Cook, stirring, for approximately 5 minutes.

3 Pour over 1 L/1¾ pt water and bring to the boil. Cover and simmer for 45 minutes until the chicken is tender.

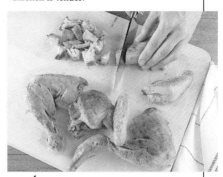

4 Using a slotted spoon, remove the chicken and cut the flesh from the bones and dice it into small pieces. Return the meat to the casserole and cook for 5 minutes to heat through. Taste and adjust the seasoning. Serve immediately while still hot.

Arcadian potato salad

Boil 700 g/1 lb 8 oz potatoes and dice when cooked. Hard boil 2 eggs and chop them up. Seed and dice 1 green pepper. Slice 2 gherkins, a bunch of spring onions and 10 stuffed green olives. Mix all these together. Mix 1 tbls Dijon mustard with 225 g/8 oz mayonnaise. Pour over the potatoes, season and toss the ingredients together. Sprinkle over freshly chopped parsley and chill for 30 minutes.

TIP
THE OKRA SHOULD BE SMALL AND TENDER. IF YOU ARE ONLY ABLE TO FIND LARGER OKRA, SLICE THEM.

MINI GALANTINES

Alan Newnham

To create these attractive cross-sections when
sliced, the chicken galantines are stuffed with
sausagemeat, pistachios and beans.

PREPARATION TIME: 40 MINS
+ COOLING
COOKING TIME: 30-35 MINS
SERVES 4

INGREDIENTS

4 CHICKEN LEGS, BONED

25 G/1 OZ FRENCH BEANS, TOPPED
AND TAILED

225 G/8 OZ PORK SAUSAGEMEAT

15 G/½ OZ PISTACHIO NUTS

½ CLOVE OF GARLIC, CRUSHED

SALT AND GROUND BLACK PEPPER

BUTTER, FOR GREASING

ORANGE SLICES, TO GARNISH

FLAT-LEAVED PARSLEY SPRIGS, TO
GARNISH

ORANGE AND LAMB'S LETTUCE
SALAD, TO SERVE

3 Mix the sausagemeat, pistachio nuts, garlic and salt and pepper together in a bowl, then divide the mixture into four. Place along the centre of the chicken legs, then lay the beans on top. Roll up carefully, making sure the beans and stuffing mixture are completely covered by the chicken.

4 Wrap the stuffed legs in 4 pieces of greased foil. Place them in a baking tin and bake for 30-35 minutes or until cooked (push a skewer into the thickest part and check that the juices that run out are clear).

1 Preheat the oven to 200 C/400 F/ Gas 6. Open out the boned chicken legs and place them, one at a time, between two sheets of cling film. Beat each leg gently with a rolling pin to flatten to a uniform thickness.

2 Blanch the beans in boiling water for 2-3 minutes to soften slightly, then drain.

 FREEZE THE UNCOOKED GALANTINES IN A RIGID CONTAINER FOR UP TO 3 MONTHS. THAW BEFORE COOKING.

5 Allow the chicken to cool, then slice. Garnish with orange slices and flat-leaved parsley and serve with the salad.

COQ AU VIN

Peter Reilly

One of the all-time classics of French country cooking, this casserole makes a nourishing family meal.

PREPARATION TIME: 15 MINS
COOKING TIME: 1¾-2¼ HOURS
SERVES 4

INGREDIENTS

1.4 KG/3 LB CHICKEN, CUT INTO 8
JOINTS

100 G/4 OZ PIECE OF UNSMOKED
BACON, CUT INTO CUBES

50 G/2 OZ BUTTER

225 G/8 OZ BABY ONIONS

50 ML/2 FL OZ BRANDY

600 ML/1 PT FULL-BODIED RED WINE
(BURGUNDY)

2 CLOVES OF GARLIC, CRUSHED

1 FRESH BOUQUET GARNI
(PARSLEY, THYME & A BAY LEAF)

1 TBLS TOMATO PUREE

SALT AND GROUND BLACK PEPPER

225 G/8 OZ BUTTON MUSHROOMS

2 TBLS FLOUR

CROUTONS, TO GARNISH

FRESHLY CHOPPED PARSLEY, TO
GARNISH

2 Cover the casserole dish and bring to the boil. Reduce the heat and simmer for 1½-2 hours until the chicken is very tender. Stir in the button mushrooms in the last 30 minutes.

3 Take out the bouquet garni. Mix the flour with the remaining 25 g/ 1 oz butter to form a paste and gradually whisk into the casserole until the cooking liquid thickens. Simmer for a further 5 minutes then serve with croûtons and freshly chopped parsley.

BOILED NEW POTATOES OR
ROAST POTATOES ARE IDEAL
TO SERVE WITH THIS DISH. A
GREEN VEGETABLE CAN BE
OPTIONAL AS THERE ARE
PLENTY OF VEGETABLES IN
THE SAUCE.

1 Sauté the chicken and bacon in half the butter in a flameproof casserole dish. When they start to brown, add the onions. Stir well then pour in the brandy and ignite. When the flames have died down add the burgundy, crushed garlic, bouquet garni and tomato purée and season with salt and pepper.

CRAYFISH CHICKEN

Hilary Moore

Enjoy the rich bounties of land and sea in this
unusual special-occasion combination
of chicken and crayfish.

PREPARATION TIME: 15 MINS
COOKING TIME: 40-50 MINS
SERVES 4

INGREDIENTS

1.4 KG/3 LB ROASTING CHICKEN

3 TBLS OIL

25 G/1 OZ BUTTER

8 RAW CRAYFISH

2 TBLS COGNAC

3 SHALLOTS, CHOPPED

1 CLOVE OF GARLIC, CRUSHED

25 G/1 OZ FLOUR

1 TBLS TOMATO PUREE

300 ML/½ PT WHITE BURGUNDY WINE

300 ML/½ PT CHICKEN STOCK

FRESH BOUQUET GARNI

50 ML/2 FL OZ DOUBLE CREAM

SALT AND GROUND BLACK PEPPER

SPRIGS OF FLAT-LEAVED PARSLEY, TO GARNISH

the chicken to the pan, simmer for 30 minutes until tender.

3 Add the crayfish and simmer for a few minutes to heat through. Then remove chicken and crayfish and keep warm. Boil the sauce vigorously for a few minutes, then stir in the cream. Add salt and pepper to taste. Spoon the sauce over the chicken and crayfish. Garnish.

1 Cut the chicken into 8 pieces. Heat the oil and butter in a flameproof casserole. Cook the crayfish over a high heat until they turn red. Pour over the cognac and flame. Transfer the crayfish to a plate. Add the chicken and cook until brown. Remove and set aside.

2 Stir in the shallots and garlic and cook until soft. Stir in the flour, tomato purée, wine, stock and bouquet garni. Bring to the boil. Return

Accompaniments

Fleshy, stalked leaves called blettes in France are better known as Swiss chard in England. As they taste rather bland, they're served with fresh herbs or in a creamy sauce. Slice and cook 450 g/1 lb with a handful of sorrel leaves in chicken stock until tender. Drain and serve hot, tossed in butter and black pepper and scattered with chopped fresh herbs.

To make artichokes with toma-toes, peel 700 g/1 lb 8 oz Jerusalem artichokes. Simmer in boiling water with a squeeze of lemon juice until just tender. Drain and slice very thickly. Heat a little oil in a pan. Add the artichokes, 4 skin-ned and chopped tomatoes, 1 tbls chopped marjoram, ground black pepper to taste. Cook very gently for 5 minutes and then serve while still piping hot.

CHICKEN WITH JUNIPER

Alan Newnham

Make good use of cheaper poultry joints with this flavoursome casserole, topped with crisp potatoes. Serve with carrots and French beans.

PREPARATION TIME: 20 MINS
COOKING TIME: 2¾ HOURS
SERVES 6-8

I N G R E D I E N T S

25 G/1 OZ BUTTER

8 CHICKEN THIGHS OR 1.8 KG/4 LB
CHICKEN JOINTS

900 G/2 LB SMALL POTATOES

SALT AND GROUND BLACK PEPPER

2 TBLS ROUGHLY CHOPPED
FRESH PARSLEY

2 TSP FRESH THYME, CHOPPED

12 JUNIPER BERRIES, CRUSHED

1 LARGE CLOVE OF GARLIC, CRUSHED

450 ML/¾ PT CHICKEN STOCK

FRESH THYME SPRIGS, TO GARNISH

3 Preheat the oven to 160 C/300 F/ Gas 2. Place the chicken on the potatoes in the casserole. Sprinkle over the remaining thyme. Cover with the rest of the potatoes. Scatter the juniper berries and garlic over the slices. Season with salt and pepper.

1 Gently melt butter in a frying-pan. Dip a brush into the butter and brush over the inside of a 1.7 L/ 3 pt casserole dish. Add the chicken to the remaining butter in the frying-pan. Sauté until evenly browned.

2 Meanwhile peel the potatoes and slice them thinly. Put half of them into the bottom of the casserole and season with salt and pepper. Add half the parsley and thyme.

4 Pour in the fat from the frying-pan and the chicken stock. Cover and cook in the oven for 2½ hours. Remove the lid after 2 hours to allow the top to brown. Remove any excess fat by blotting the potatoes with kitchen paper. Scatter the reserved parsley over the top. Garnish with thyme and serve.

TRY THIS DISH WITH A GLASS OF A LIGHT RED WINE, LIKE BEAUJOLAIS.

TIP

TRY THE SCOTTISH VERSION — LEAVE OUT THE JUNIPER BERRIES AND ADD ONIONS TO THE POTATOES.

ZESTY CHICKEN

Hilary Moore

The tangy juice of fresh oranges and lemons gives everyday chicken portions a refreshing lift.

PREPARATION TIME: 15 MINS
COOKING TIME: 1 HOUR
SERVES 6

INGREDIENTS

6 CHICKEN PORTIONS
2 CLOVES OF GARLIC, CRUSHED
½ TSP GROUND CINNAMON
½ TSP GROUND GINGER
SALT AND GROUND BLACK PEPPER
2 TBLS OIL
1 TBLS GRATED ORANGE ZEST
1 TSP GRATED LEMON ZEST
JUICE OF 2 ORANGES
JUICE OF 1 LEMON
1 TBLS HONEY
1 TBLS FINELY CHOPPED FRESH ROOT GINGER
175 ML/6 FL OZ CHICKEN STOCK
1 TBLS CORNFLOUR
1 ORANGE, SLICED, TO GARNISH

1 Wash and dry the chicken portions, then add garlic, cinnamon, ginger and seasoning.

2 Preheat the oven to 190 C/375 F/ Gas 5. Heat the oil in a large frying-pan. Add the chicken in batches and fry over a moderate heat for 10 minutes, turning frequently. Transfer the chicken to an ovenproof casserole using a fish slice or slotted spoon.

3 Pour the fat from the cooking juices into a saucepan and add the zest and juice from the oranges and lemon, honey, ginger and stock. Bring to the boil and simmer for 3 minutes. Pour over the the chicken portions. Place the casserole in the preheated oven and bake for 40 minutes.

4 Transfer the chicken to a warmed serving dish. Strain the cooking liquid through a sieve into a small pan. Mix the cornflour with 1 tbls water until it becomes a smooth paste and add to the pan to thicken. Bring to the boil then simmer for 1-2 minutes, stirring constantly until the sauce has thickened. Pour over the chicken portions in the dish. Garnish with the orange slices and serve immediately.

TIP

THIS CHICKEN DISH CAN BE FROZEN BUT EAT IT WITHIN 3 MONTHS.

ITALIAN-STYLE CHICKEN

Clint Brown

This oven-cooked chicken is served with grilled Mozzarella – the cheese traditionally used in pizzas – melting over the top.

PREPARATION TIME: 5 MINS
COOKING TIME: 1 HOUR
SERVES 4

I N G R E D I E N T S

4 LARGE CHICKEN BREASTS, SKINNED

2 CLOVES OF GARLIC, CRUSHED

2 TSP CHOPPED TARRAGON

SALT AND GROUND BLACK PEPPER

15 G/½ OZ BUTTER

3 TBLS OIL

1 ONION, FINELY CHOPPED

2 SHALLOTS, FINELY CHOPPED

400 G/14 OZ TINNED TOMATOES,
CHOPPED

2 TBLS TOMATO PUREE

2 TSP SUGAR

1 TSP OREGANO

150 ML/¼ PT CHICKEN STOCK

150 G/5 OZ MOZZARELLA CHEESE,
SLICED

BLACK OLIVES AND MINT, TO
GARNISH

2 Heat the remaining oil in a saucepan, add the onion and shallots and fry for 5 minutes. Add the tomatoes, tomato purée, sugar, oregano and chicken stock. Season to taste with salt and pepper and cook for 15 minutes over low heat.

3 Preheat the oven to 180 C/350 F/ Gas 4. Spoon the tomato sauce over the chicken breasts, cover with foil and place in the oven. Cook for 25 minutes.

1 Season the chicken breasts with the garlic, tarragon, salt and pepper. Melt the butter and 1 tbls oil in a frying-pan and gently fry the chicken for 3 minutes on each side. Transfer to a flameproof dish.

TIP

IF YOU CAN'T BUY MOZZARELLA TRY USING GOUDA OR GRUYERE INSTEAD.

4 Set the grill to high. Remove the chicken from the oven and cover with the sliced mozzarella cheese. Place under the grill for 3-5 minutes, or until the cheese has melted. Garnish with olives and mint leaves and serve.

COUNTRY CHICKEN BAKE

Clint Brown

This country chicken bake is the perfect dish for large numbers. Simply double or treble the quantities and cook in roasting tins covered with foil.

PREPARATION TIME: 15 MINS
COOKING TIME: 1 HOUR 10 MINS
SERVES 4-6

INGREDIENTS

| 10 CHICKEN THIGHS, BONED |
| 2 TBLS SEASONED FLOUR |
| 2 TBLS OIL |
| 1 ONION, SLICED |
| 4 CELERY STALKS, SLICED |
| 225 G/8 OZ POTATO, PEELED AND DICED |
| 350 G/12 OZ TOMATOES, QUARTERED |
| 2 TSP CHOPPED FRESH PARSLEY |
| 2 TSP CHOPPED FRESH THYME |
| 300 ML/½ PT CHICKEN STOCK |
| SALT AND GROUND BLACK PEPPER |
| 2 TSP CORNFLOUR |

2 Top the chicken with the celery, potato and tomatoes. Add the parsley and thyme.

3 Pour the chicken stock into the casserole and season. Cover with the lid and place in the oven for 45 minutes. Remove the dish from the oven. Blend the cornflour with a little water, stir into the casserole, then return to the oven, covered with the lid for a further 10-15 minutes.

1 Preheat the oven to 180 C/350 F/ Gas 4. Coat the chicken in the flour, tap to remove excess. Heat the oil in a frying-pan, add the onion and fry for 2-3 minutes. Remove from the pan and place in a casserole dish. Add the chicken to the oil and fry in batches to brown all sides. Place the chicken on top of the onions in the dish.

 SERVE WITH WILD RICE, LONG-GRAIN RICE AND PINE KERNELS. GARNISH WITH CELERY LEAVES.

BAKED CHICKEN PARCELS

Vegetables and chicken breasts cooked in paper parcels are economical and straightforward to make. They are also the perfect dish for health-conscious slimmers who want flavour as well as low calories.

PREPARATION TIME: 25 MINS
COOKING TIME: 40 MINS
SERVES 4

INGREDIENTS

| 1 LEEK |
| 2 LARGE CARROTS, PEELED |
| 2 CELERY STALKS, TRIMMED |
| 1 PARSNIP, PEELED |
| 4 SMALL CHICKEN BREAST FILLETS, SKINNED |
| 4 SPRIGS FRESH TARRAGON |
| 25 G/1 OZ BUTTER |
| 125 ML/4 FL OZ WHITE WINE |

each with a knob of butter. Fold over the circle and seal the edges by twisting the paper. Leave a small opening. Place the parcels in a baking dish.

 Pour the wine into the parcels and twist to seal up the opening. Place in the oven and bake for 40 minutes or until cooked through.

 BAKED CHICKEN PARCELS ARE DELICIOUS SERVED WITH BOILED OR SAUTE POTATOES.

m PLACE THE PARCELS IN A SHALLOW MICROWAVE-PROOF DISH. COOK ON HIGH (100%) FOR 11-13 MINUTES. LEAVE TO STAND FOR 5 MINUTES BEFORE SERVING.

1 Preheat oven to 190 C/375 F/ Gas 5. Cut the leek, carrots, celery and parsnip into 7.5 cm/3 in matchsticks. Cut out 4 × 20 cm/8 in circles of greaseproof paper.

2 Place a chicken breast on each greaseproof paper circle. Top with a mixture of the finely cut vegetables and a sprig of tarragon. Dot

CHICKEN KIEV

Alan Newnham

Chicken Kiev originated in the Ukraine but seems to be at home almost anywhere. Here's a simple variation with herbs and lemon juice which is excellent served with a glass of your favourite white wine.

PREPARATION TIME: 35 MINS +
CHILLING
COOKING TIME: 12-16 MINS
SERVES 4

INGREDIENTS

4 LARGE SKINNED AND BONED
CHICKEN BREASTS, PREFERABLY
WITH WING BONES ATTACHED

SUNFLOWER OIL, FOR DEEP FRYING

PARSLEY SPRIGS, TO GARNISH

LEMON SLICES, TO GARNISH

GREEN SALAD, TO SERVE

FOR THE HERB BUTTER

75 G/3 OZ BUTTER, SOFTENED

GRATED ZEST AND JUICE OF ½ A
LEMON

1 TBLS CHOPPED FRESH PARSLEY

1 TSP CHOPPED FRESH TARRAGON

1 TSP CHOPPED FRESH CHIVES

1 CLOVE OF GARLIC, CRUSHED

GROUND BLACK PEPPER

FOR THE COATING

1 EGG

1 TSP SUNFLOWER OIL

SEASONED FLOUR

75 G/3 OZ WHITE BREADCRUMBS

2 Place the chicken breasts between two sheets of cling film and beat out firmly but gently with a heavy rolling-pin until flattened.

3 Place a stick of herb butter in the centre and fold the meat over, tucking in the edges to completely enclose it. Repeat with other sticks.

4 Make the coating: beat the egg with 1 tsp water and the sunflower oil. Dust the chicken breasts with the seasoned flour, then dip in the egg mixture and coat with the breadcrumbs, pressing on well. Chill for 30 minutes, then dip in egg and breadcrumbs a second time. Chill, uncovered, for 3 hours or overnight.

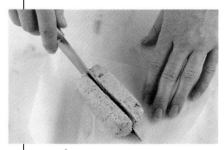

1 Blend the softened butter with the lemon zest and juice, the herbs, garlic and pepper. Shape into a 5 x 2.5 cm/2 x 1 in rectangle, place on greaseproof paper and chill until firm. Cut into 4 long sticks and freeze for 1 hour.

5 Heat the oil in a deep fat fryer to 180 C/350 F and fry the chicken breasts, two at a time, for 6-8 minutes or until golden brown. Drain on kitchen paper and keep warm while frying the remaining chicken breasts. Garnish the chicken with parsley and lemon slices and serve with salad leaves.

SAVOURY STUFFED CHICKEN BREASTS

Peter Reilly

Chicken breasts are perfect for stuffing. This flavoursome filling is a combination of leeks, pine kernels and breadcrumbs.

PREPARATION TIME: 10 MINS
COOKING TIME: 45 MINS
SERVES 4

INGREDIENTS

4 BONED CHICKEN BREASTS

40 G/1 ½ OZ BUTTER, PLUS EXTRA
FOR GREASING

FOR THE STUFFING

1 LEEK, FINELY SLICED

3 TBLS FRESH BROWN
BREADCRUMBS

1 TBLS PINE KERNELS

1 EGG YOLK

1 TBLS FINELY CHOPPED PARSLEY

SALT AND GROUND BLACK PEPPER

100 G/4 OZ EDAM OR GOUDA CHEESE,
GRATED

JUICE AND FINELY GRATED ZEST OF
½ A LEMON

FOR THE GARNISH

SPRIGS OF WATERCRESS

WEDGES OF LEMON

2 Melt 15 g/½ oz butter in a frying-pan and sauté the leek for 2 minutes to soften.

3 Remove the frying-pan from the heat. Add the breadcrumbs, pine kernels, egg yolk, parsley, seasoning and the grated cheese. Then mix in the lemon juice and zest.

4 Spoon the stuffing into each of the chicken breasts and transfer to a buttered ovenproof dish.

1 Preheat the oven to 200 C/400 F/ Gas 6. Carefully cut a pocket in each side of the chicken breasts using a sharp kitchen knife.

 SERVE WITH A SELECTION OF FRESH VEGETABLES, LIKE CARROTS AND BOILED NEW POTATOES.

5 Dot the breasts with the remaining butter. Bake in the oven for 35-40 minutes, basting occasionally. Garnish with watercress and lemon.

PEPPERED CHICKEN

Hilary Moore

Peppered chicken is a feast for all the senses,
tantalising the tastebuds and delighting the eye.

PREPARATION TIME: 15 MINS
+ MARINATING
COOKING TIME: 45-50 MINS
SERVES 4

INGREDIENTS

4 CHICKEN PORTIONS

1 TSP GOLDEN GRANULATED SUGAR

2 TSP WHOLE BLACK PEPPERCORNS

2 CLOVES OF GARLIC

75 ML/3 FL OZ TOMATO KETCHUP

1 TBLS WORCESTERSHIRE SAUCE

1 TBLS WHITE WINE VINEGAR

1 TBLS FRENCH DIJON MUSTARD

SALT

LONG GRAIN RICE, TO SERVE

BROCCOLI, TO SERVE

2 Pour the marinade over the chicken in a glass, glazed earthenware or ovenproof dish. Turn the chicken portions over to coat thoroughly with the marinade. Cover with foil and leave to marinate for several hours in a cool place or fridge. Preheat oven to 190 C/375 F/Gas 5.

1 Wipe chicken portions, then slash the fleshy part several times with a sharp knife. Sprinkle with sugar which will release the juices. Crush peppercorns coarsely in a pestle and mortar or between sheets of greaseproof paper in a teatowel. Add garlic, ketchup, Worcestershire sauce, vinegar, mustard and salt.

3 Turn the pieces of chicken in the marinade, then cook for 35-40 minutes. Remove foil and cook for a further 8-10 minutes until they are a rich colour and cooked through. Serve hot with freshly cooked rice and broccoli.

TIP

TO COOK THESE CHICKEN PORTIONS OVER A BARBECUE, DRIZZLE THEM WITH A LITTLE OIL AND THEN PLACE ON A RACK OVER HOT COALS FOR 10-15 MINUTES.

CHICKEN PIRI-PIRI

Clint Brown

Piri-piri is a spicy Portuguese-African sauce similar to Tabasco. It is sold bottled but is difficult to get hold of, so here is a chicken recipe with a do-it-yourself sauce.

PREPARATION TIME: 20 MINS
COOKING TIME: 1 ½ HOURS
SERVES 6

I N G R E D I E N T S

3 TBLS OIL

6 CHICKEN BREASTS, SKINNED

2 ONIONS, SLICED INTO RINGS

6 TOMATOES, CHOPPED

1 LARGE PARSNIP, CUT INTO STICKS

2 CARROTS, CUT INTO STICKS

1 CINNAMON STICK

SALT AND GROUND BLACK PEPPER

2-3 TBLS HOMEMADE OR 1-2 TBLS
READY-MADE PIRI-PIRI SAUCE

1 LARGE RED PEPPER

1 LARGE YELLOW PEPPER

FOR THE PIRI-PIRI SAUCE

JUICE OF 2 LEMONS

½ RED PEPPER, SEEDED AND SLICED

4 HOT RED CHILLIES, SEEDED AND
SLICED

1 TBLS OLIVE OIL

PINCH OF SALT

2 Heat the oil in a large flameproof casserole or large frying-pan and brown the chicken breasts in batches if necessary. Add the onions, tomatoes, parsnip, carrots, cinnamon stick, salt and pepper and 750 ml/1¼ pt water. Bring to the boil and stir in 1 tbls of the piri-piri sauce. Cover and simmer gently for 30 minutes.

3 Halve the peppers, remove the seeds and then slice thinly. Add to the pan and simmer, covered, for a further 30 minutes or until the peppers and other vegetables are tender.

4 Using a slotted spoon, transfer the chicken and vegetables to a serving dish and keep warm. Stir a further 1 tbls piri-piri sauce into the liquid in the pan (less if you're using ready-made sauce). Taste and add another 1 tbls sauce if necessary. Bring to the boil and then cook rapidly until reduced by about a third. Pour over the chicken and vegetables or serve separately.

1 First make the piri-piri sauce: place the lemon juice in a saucepan with the red pepper and chillies. Bring to the boil, then cover and simmer gently for 10-15 minutes or until the peppers are tender. Place in a food processor or blender and purée to a thick paste. Add the oil and salt.

CHICKEN CREOLE

To allow the flavours of this dish to mature,
make it the day before and reheat when required.

PREPARATION TIME: 10 MINS
+ MARINATING
COOKING TIME: 1 ¼-1 ½ HOURS
SERVES 6

INGREDIENTS

6 CHICKEN LEG PORTIONS, HALVED
4 TBLS DARK RUM
2 IN PIECE FRESH ROOT GINGER, PEELED AND GRATED
2 TSP GROUND MACE
GRATED ZEST OF ½ LEMON
JUICE OF 1 LEMON
1 TSP SALT
DASH OF TABASCO
1 TSP MUSCOVADO SUGAR
3 CLOVES OF GARLIC, CRUSHED
40 G/1 ½ OZ BUTTER
1 ½ TBLS OIL
1 ONION, FINELY CHOPPED
½ TSP GROUND ALLSPICE
2 TBLS TOMATO PUREE
300 ML/½ PT STRONG CHICKEN STOCK
25 G/1 OZ CREAMED COCONUT
SALT AND GROUND BLACK PEPPER
CHOPPED PARSLEY, TO GARNISH

over the chicken, mix well, cover and set aside in a cool place for at least 4 hours or overnight, if possible.

2 Heat the butter and oil in a flameproof casserole. Shake off the excess marinade and fry the chicken on all sides until richly browned. Remove to a plate. Add the onion and remaining garlic to the pan and sauté for 5 minutes. Stir in the remaining rum, ginger and mace, the allspice and tomato purée, any remaining marinade and the stock. Return the chicken to the pan, cover and cook over a gentle heat for 1 hour or until the chicken is tender.

3 Stir in the creamed coconut and if the sauce is too liquid, simmer uncovered until thickened. Check the seasoning, garnish with the chopped parsley and serve with Riz Creole.

Riz Creole

Wash 350 g/12 oz American long-grain rice under cold running water until the water runs clear. Put the rice, 1½ tsp salt and 900ml/1½ pt water into a pan, bring to the boil, cover and cook over a low heat for 12-15 minutes. Drain and rinse the cooked rice in cold water. Drain, put rice back into the pan and dry it out, uncovered, over a low heat for 5 minutes.

1 Put the chicken in a casserole. In a jug mix together half the rum, half the ginger, half the mace, the lemon zest and juice of one lemon, salt, Tabasco, sugar and 1 clove of garlic. Pour

CHICKEN & COCONUT CURRY

James Duncan

Succulent chicken portions in a creamy tomato
sauce are flavoured with Indian spices.
What could be better than this spicy chicken
and coconut curry served on a bed of rice for a
special mid-week meal?

PREPARATION TIME: 10 MINS

COOKING TIME: 1 HOUR-1 HOUR 20 MINS

SERVES 4

INGREDIENTS

1 TSP SALT
3 TSP TURMERIC
1 TBLS FLOUR
1.4 KG/3 LB CHICKEN, CUT INTO 8 PIECES
4 TBLS VEGETABLE OIL
1 LARGE ONION, SLICED
2 CLOVES OF GARLIC, CRUSHED
5 CM/2 IN PIECE FRESH GINGER, GRATED
2 GREEN CHILLIES, SLICED
3 TSP GROUND CORIANDER
1½ TSP GROUND CUMIN
2 TSP GARAM MASALA
1 TSP GROUND CINNAMON
400 G/14 OZ TINNED TOMATOES, CHOPPED
125 ML/4 FL OZ CHICKEN STOCK
2 TBLS CREAMED COCONUT
SALT AND GROUND BLACK PEPPER
1 TBLS FRESHLY CHOPPED CORIANDER, TO GARNISH

saucepan. Add the chicken and fry, turning regularly until golden on all sides. Remove the chicken and set aside.

2 Add the onion to the pan and cook gently for about 5 minutes. Add the garlic, ginger, chillies, coriander, cumin, garam masala, cinnamon and 2 tbls water. Cook for 3 minutes stirring frequently. Add the tomatoes and stock, bring to the boil then add the chicken pieces. Cover and simmer for 40-50 minutes until the chicken is tender.

3 Stir in the creamed coconut and simmer for a further 5 minutes. Season with the salt and ground black pepper, sprinkle with the chopped coriander and serve.

1 Mix the salt, turmeric and flour together on a plate. Turn the chicken pieces in the mixture to coat. Heat the oil in a large heavy-based

TO SET THE SCENE, SERVE THIS CURRY WITH BOWLS OF MANGO CHUTNEY, YOGHURT, FINELY CHOPPED CUCUMBER AND BOILED RICE.

AROMATIC CHICKEN

Clint Brown

Fresh coriander and tumeric give this chicken
recipe its distinctive flavour and colour.

PREPARATION TIME: 10 MINS
COOKING TIME: 35-40 MINS
SERVES 4

INGREDIENTS

1.4 KG/3 LB CHICKEN JOINTS

½ TSP GROUND TURMERIC

1 TSP SALT

4 WHOLE CARDAMOM PODS

5 TBLS OIL

2 MEDIUM ONIONS, SLICED

3 WHOLE CLOVES

5 BLACK PEPPERCORNS

4 CM/1 ½ IN CINNAMON STICK

3 CLOVES OF GARLIC, CRUSHED

600 ML/1 PT SET YOGHURT

100 G/4 OZ CORIANDER, CHOPPED

GROUND BLACK PEPPER

3 Remove the chicken pieces and boil the liquid rapidly to reduce by half. Add the liquid to the yoghurt and strain to remove the spices.

4 Return the chicken to the pan with the yoghurt sauce and onions. Cover and simmer gently to heat the chicken through. Stir in the fresh chopped coriander and pepper.

1 Put the chicken joints into a pan with the ground turmeric, salt, whole cardamom pods and 600 ml/1 pt water. Bring to the boil, cover and simmer for 20 minutes until the meat is tender. Meanwhile, heat the oil in a large frying-pan and cook the onions gently until golden brown all over. Remove onions from the pan with a slotted spoon.

2 Put the whole cloves, black peppercorns, and cinnamon into the same oil, add the crushed garlic and yoghurt and cook gently to make a thick white sauce.

TIP

WHEN COOKING THE YOGHURT TO A THICK SAUCE MAKE SURE YOU DON'T HEAT IT TOO FIERCELY OR YOU MAY FIND THE YOGHURT WILL CURDLE. TO PREVENT THIS, ADD A LITTLE CORNFLOUR BLENDED WITH COLD WATER TO THE YOGHURT BEFORE COOKING.

CRISPY STUFFED CHICKEN

Slice into these chicken breasts, with their crunchy breadcrumb coating, and a tasty spinach filling will ooze out. Serve with salad leaves and chilled white wine.

PREPARATION TIME: 20 MINS
+ CHILLING
COOKING TIME: 15 MINS
SERVES 4

INGREDIENTS

4 CHICKEN BREASTS, SKINNED

100 G/4 OZ DRIED WHITE
BREADCRUMBS

1 LARGE EGG, BEATEN

OIL, FOR DEEP FRYING

LEMON SLICES, TO GARNISH

FOR THE FILLING

300 G/12 OZ FROZEN CHOPPED
SPINACH, THAWED AND SQUEEZED
UNTIL THOROUGHLY DRY

75 G/3 OZ RICOTTA CHEESE

4 TBLS GRATED PARMESAN

1 TSP DIJON MUSTARD

4 TBLS CHOPPED FRESH PARSLEY

GRATED ZEST OF ½ A LEMON

SALT AND GROUND BLACK PEPPER

3 Shake the dried breadcrumbs onto a baking tray. Taking one chicken breast at a time, dip completely into the beaten egg and coat one side with the breadcrumbs. Spoon 1-2 tbls of the spinach filling down the centre of each breast leaving a good 12 mm/½ in edge clear of the mixture.

1 Take each chicken breast in turn and lay on a board. Using a sharp knife, cut the breast horizontally along one side almost through to the other side, then open the breasts out and set them aside.

2 For the filling: press the excess water out of the spinach. Add to the béchamel, with the other filling ingredients. Season to taste.

4 Fold over one side to cover the filling and press the edges together well. Spoon some more breadcrumbs over the breast and press them down, so that they are well-coated. Lift them onto a plate and chill in the fridge for 30 minutes.

5 Heat the oil to 180 C/350 F and deep fry the chicken in 2 batches for 3 minutes on each side. Drain on kitchen paper and keep the first batch hot in a low oven while you cook the second batch.

PIQUANT CHICKEN

Michael Michaels

The chicken for this Chinese-inspired meal is steamed whole, then deep fried and served with a thick, spicy sauce.

PREPARATION TIME: 25 MINS
+ STANDING
COOKING TIME: 1 ¼ HOURS
SERVES 6

INGREDIENTS

2.5 CM/1 IN PIECE ROOT GINGER,
PEELED AND CUT INTO STRIPS

3 SPRING ONIONS, SLICED

1.4 KG/3 LB OVEN-READY CHICKEN

OIL, FOR DEEP FRYING

FOR THE SAUCE

1 TSP CORNFLOUR

3 CLOVES OF GARLIC, CRUSHED

2 TBLS RICE WINE VINEGAR

6 TBLS LIGHT SOY SAUCE

2 SPRING ONIONS,
FINELY CHOPPED

2 TSP CASTER SUGAR

1 Mix together the strips of ginger and sliced spring onions and place in the cavity of the chicken. Cover and leave to stand at room temperature for 30 minutes.

2 Put the chicken on a plate and place in a large bamboo steamer set over a wok ¼ full with boiling water. Reduce the heat under the wok, cover and steam for 1 hour or until the juices run clear when the chicken is pierced in the thickest part of the leg. Top up the water as required.

3 Remove the chicken and place on a wire rack and allow to cool, uncovered, for 3-4 hours. Cut the chicken in half lengthways.

4 Heat the oil to 180 C/350 F in a deep fat fryer and cook half the chicken at a time, for 5-7 minutes, until golden and crispy. Drain on kitchen paper. Cut off large pieces of meat and arrange on a serving platter.

5 Make the sauce, place the cornflour in small pan and stir in remaining sauce ingredients and heat slowly, stirring until thickened. Pour over the chicken and serve with the Broccoli salad.

Broccoli salad

Cut 450 g/1 lb of broccoli into spears and slice the broccoli stems. Blanch the heads and stems in boiling water for 4-5 minutes. Plunge into cold water, then drain well and place in a salad bowl. Toast 2 tbls sesame seeds until golden and then mix them with 1 tbls sesame oil, 1 tbls corn oil, 1 crushed clove of garlic, 2 tbls light soy sauce and 2 tbls chopped spring onions. Pour the dressing over the broccoli and toss well. Serve immediately.

FRENCH ROAST CHICKEN

Diana Miller

This succulent French Roast Chicken is simple
to make and can be served with potatoes and
buttered whole carrots for an unusual
family Sunday roast.

PREPARATION TIME: 15 MINS
COOKING TIME: 1¼ HOURS
SERVES 4-6

I N G R E D I E N T S

15 G/½ OZ BUTTER

1 TBLS VEGETABLE OIL

1.6 KG/3 LB 8 OZ WHOLE CHICKEN

CELERY SALT

GROUND BLACK PEPPER

2 CLOVES OF GARLIC, PEELED

12 ROSEMARY SPRIGS

12 THYME SPRIGS

150 ML/¼ PT CHICKEN STOCK

3 TBLS DOUBLE CREAM

2 Season the chicken with the celery salt and pepper. Tuck the cloves of garlic and about 4 sprigs of both rosemary and thyme under the legs. Pour 50 ml/2 fl oz of the chicken stock over the chicken, cover and cook for 45 minutes. Uncover and cook for a further 15 minutes.

3 Remove from the oven, transfer the chicken to a warmed serving dish and keep warm in a low oven while you prepare the sauce.

1 Preheat the oven to 200 C/400 F/ Gas 6. Melt the butter with the oil in a large frying-pan, add the chicken and cook, turning constantly, for 5 minutes or until golden brown. Transfer to a medium-sized casserole dish. Reserve the cooking juices in the frying-pan.

4 Strain the juices from the casserole into the frying-pan. Pour in the reserved stock and bring to the boil, stirring constantly. Continue boiling until it is reduced by half then allow it to cool slightly before stirring in the cream. Serve the chicken surrounded by the remaining thyme and rosemary sprigs with the sauce served separately in a small sauce boat.

TIP

WHEN YOU POUR IN THE COLD STOCK ADD 2 TBLS WHITE WINE OR BRANDY AT THE SAME TIME FOR A RICHER FLAVOUR.

CAJUN ROAST CHICKEN

Clint Brown

Cajun is a robust style of cookery, originally from the Deep South of the United States. The full, spicy flavour of this recipe is typical of Cajun cooking.

PREPARATION TIME: 25 MINS
COOKING TIME: 1 ½-1 ¾ HOURS
SERVES 6

I N G R E D I E N T S

1.4 KG/3 LB CHICKEN
3 TBLS SEASONED FLOUR
4 TBLS OIL
1 ONION, CHOPPED
350 G/12 OZ OKRA, TRIMMED AND CUT INTO CHUNKS
150 G/5 OZ CHORIZO SAUSAGE, SLICED INTO 6 MM/¼ IN PIECES
2 CLOVES OF GARLIC, CRUSHED
2.5 CM/1 IN PIECE OF FRESH ROOT GINGER, GRATED
400 G/14 OZ TINNED TOMATOES
RICE, TO SERVE

2 Cook the onion, okra and sausage gently for 3 minutes in the same pan. Add the garlic and ginger and cook for a further 5 minutes. Stir in 1 tbls of the reserved flour to absorb the oil, and then add the tomatoes. Bring to the boil, stirring continuously.

3 Place the mixture in a casserole. Lay the chicken on top and cover tightly with a lid or foil. Place in the oven and cook for 1¼-1½ hours until tender. Serve the chicken on top of the tomato mixture with rice.

 REMOVE THE MEAT FROM THE COOKED CHICKEN, COOL AND PACK IN FOIL CONTAINERS WITH THE VEGETABLE MIXTURE. LABEL AND FREEZE. USE WITHIN 3 MONTHS. THAW AND THEN HEAT ON TOP OF THE COOKER IN A PAN.

1 Preheat the oven to 180 C/350 F/ Gas 4. Coat the chicken in the flour, reserving excess. Heat the oil in a frying-pan and brown the chicken. Remove and set aside.

TIP
OKRA SHOULD BE FIRM, BRIGHT GREEN AND UNBLEMISHED OR IT GOES SLIMY WHEN COOKED. IF YOU HAVE DIFFICULTY FINDING OKRA, USE COURGETTES INSTEAD. CHORIZO SAUSAGE TOO MAY BE DIFFICULT TO FIND, IN WHICH CASE ANY CONTINENTAL GARLIC SAUSAGE WILL SUBSTITUTE WELL.

POUSSINS WITH GRAPES

Peter Reilly

An elegant main course and just as tempting
served with vegetable purée and creamed
potatoes or fresh green salad.

PREPARATION TIME: 20 MINS
COOKING TIME: 1 HOUR 10 MINS-
1 HOUR 25 MINS
SERVES 4

I N G R E D I E N T S

50 G/2 OZ BUTTER

4 SMALL POUSSINS

4 TBLS COINTREAU

FRESH SPRIG OF THYME

4 RASHERS OF BACON, DICED

2 CLOVES OF GARLIC, CRUSHED

2 TSP CORNFLOUR

225 ML/8 FL OZ WHITE WINE

100 G/4 OZ RED SEEDLESS GRAPES

SALT AND GROUND BLACK PEPPER

FRESH THYME, TO GARNISH

3 Put the poussins into a roasting tin with any juices in the frying-pan and the fresh thyme. Cover and cook for 45 minutes-1 hour until poussins are tender. Set aside and keep warm.

4 Drain any cooking juices in the roasting tin into a saucepan. Heat until the juices have reduced and only the fat remains. Add the bacon and cook until just brown. Add the garlic and fry briefly. Blend the cornflour with a little wine, then pour into the pan with rest of the wine. Halve the grapes and add to sauce with seasoning.

1 Preheat the oven to 200 C/400 C/ Gas 6. Heat the butter in a large frying-pan. Add the poussins and cook over a high heat until golden.

5 Bring the sauce to the boil, stirring. Simmer for 5 minutes then spoon over the poussins.

TIP

IF THE POUSSINS SEEM TOO LARGE, COOK TWO, THEN CUT IN HALF DOWN THE BREAST AND BACKBONE. SERVE HALF A POUSSIN EACH.

2 Pour the Cointreau over the poussins in the pan. Ignite and heat until flames die down.

SPICED POUSSINS WITH PEACHES

Clint Brown

Sweet juicy peaches accompany succulent,
whole young chickens to create a dish that
combines sweetness and spiciness in a most
subtle and delicious way.

PREPARATION TIME: 20 MINS
COOKING TIME: 45 MINS
SERVES 4

INGREDIENTS

GRATED ZEST OF 2 LEMONS

GRATED ZEST OF 2 ORANGES

JUICE OF ½ A LEMON

1 SMALL ONION, PEELED AND
CHOPPED

1 CLOVE OF GARLIC, CRUSHED

100 G/4 OZ BUTTER, SOFTENED

1 TBLS CURRY POWDER

4 TBLS CONCENTRATED ORANGE
JUICE, THAWED IF FROZEN

SALT AND GROUND BLACK PEPPER

4 POUSSINS

25 G/1 OZ BUTTER

2 LARGE PEACHES, HALVED AND
STONED

WATERCRESS, TO GARNISH

1 Preheat the oven to 230 C/450 F/ Gas 8. Put the lemon and orange zest in a mixing bowl and pour in the lemon juice. Add the onion, garlic, butter, curry powder and concentrated orange juice. Season well with salt and pepper then beat until smooth. Chill.

2 Wipe birds inside and out. Loosen the breast skin by working fingers between skin and flesh. Smear 2 tbls orange butter under the skin of each

bird. Spread the rest on top. Save 2 tbls for the peaches. Tie the legs together. Stand on a wire rack over a roasting tin.

3 Lower the heat to 200 C/400 F/Gas 6 and put the birds into the oven. Roast for 45 minutes, basting frequently, until the leg juices run clear.

4 Dot the cut side of the peaches with the reserved butter and add to the tin about 15 minutes before the birds are cooked. Remove from oven.

5 Untie birds. Serve with peaches. Spoon the butter juices over the top. Garnish with watercress.

 SERVE WITH SLICED BOILED OR SAUTÉED COURGETTES AND OTHER SEASONAL VEGETABLES OF YOUR CHOICE.

POUSSINS STUFFED WITH RICE

Ian O'Leary

Tender young poussins make a feast for four.
These are stuffed with rice and red pepper,
roasted, then topped with melting slices of
Gruyère. Allow one per person.

PREPARATION TIME: 15 MINS
COOKING TIME: 1 HOUR
SERVES 4

INGREDIENTS

4 OVEN-READY POUSSINS

SALT AND GROUND BLACK PEPPER

100 G/4 OZ GRUYERE CHEESE

100 G/4 OZ COOKED RICE

2 TBLS PETITS POIS

½ RED PEPPER, SEEDED AND DICED

2 TBLS OIL

WATERCRESS, TO GARNISH

GRAPES, TO GARNISH

3 Brush the poussins thoroughly with oil. Roast for 1 hour. Lay the slices of cheese over the top of the birds 5 minutes before they are done. Serve on a platter, garnished with sprigs of watercress and grapes.

TIP

GRUYERE IS AN EXCELLENT MELTING CHEESE BUT IF YOU CAN'T FIND ANY, USE CHEDDAR INSTEAD.

 SERVE WITH STEAMED BROCCOLI AND MASHED POTATOES. IF YOU WANT TO SERVE WITH GRAVY, STIR 2 TSP FLOUR INTO THE ROASTING TIN AND STIR OVER A MODERATE HEAT UNTIL PALE GOLDEN IN COLOUR. GRADUALLY STIR IN 200 ML/7 FL OZ CHICKEN STOCK AND BRING TO THE BOIL. SIMMER FOR 1-2 MINUTES, ADD A KNOB OF BUTTER AND SEASON LIGHTLY.

1 Wipe the poussins inside and out then season. Grate half the cheese and slice the remainder.

2 Preheat the oven to 190 C/375 F/ Gas 5. Mix the grated cheese, rice, petits pois and pepper together. Spoon the mixture into each poussin.

INDEX